Brontë Kitchen

D1388533

Uniform with this volume:

THE DALESMAN BOOK OF COUNTRY RECIPES
TRADITIONAL YORKSHIRE RECIPES

Brontë Kitchen

Recipes from Haworth families
collected by Victoria Wright

Dalesman Books 1984

The Dalesman Publishing Company Ltd.,
Clapham, via Lancaster, LA2 8EB

First published 1984

(Many of the recipes in this book originally appeared in
"A Haworth Kitchen", published in 1981 by Watmoughs Ltd).

ISBN: 0 85206 783 6

Phototypeset, printed and bound by Galava Printing Company Limited, Nelson, Lancashire

Contents

Cover drawing by Vivien Wright
Line illustrations by the author

Introduction

Tabitha Aykroyd came to live at Haworth Parsonage in 1825 and for the next thirty years she worked for the Brontë family as their servant and cook. Her kitchen became a warm and happy place for the motherless Brontë children, a kitchen full of bustle and chatter and the smell of new baking. Charlotte, Emily and Anne liked to sit at the kitchen table, helping Tabby to peel vegetables and knead the bread, listening to the stories she told them about the people and history of Haworth.

Tabitha's cooking was plain and wholesome, using only simple ingredients and traditional methods. Her recipes would be the ones kept for generations in her own family; well-trusted recipes, handed down from mother to daughter, or exchanged between neighbours and friends.

The traditional Yorkshire recipes in this book were written down in the early nineteenth century and kept in family cookery books, now faded and fragile with age and long use. All these recipes came from Haworth families, and some will have been used by Tabitha Aykroyd during the years she spent as a cook in the Brontës' kitchen.

Meat, Poultry and Game

Mutton Hash

The following is an extract from a letter written by Charlotte Brontë in Brussels to her sister Emily in Haworth, dated 1 December 1843.

'I should like uncommonly to be in the dining-room at home, or in the kitchen, or in the back kitchen. I should like even to be cutting up the hash, with the clerk and some register people at the other table, and you standing by, watching that I put enough flour, not too much pepper, and, above all, that I save the best pieces of the leg of mutton for Tiger and Keeper, the first of which personages would be jumping about the dish and carving-knife, and the latter standing like a devouring flame on the kitchen-floor. To complete the picture, Tabby blowing the fire, in order to boil the potatoes to a sort of vegetable glue! How divine are these recollections to me at this moment!'

1lb cold cooked mutton	salt and pepper
1oz butter	2 onions
1oz flour	1 pint brown stock

Slice the meat thinly and arrange the slices in an ovenproof dish. Slice the onions, and fry them gently in the butter until soft. Stir in the flour, add the stock and boil for three minutes or until the sauce is thick. Season with salt and pepper, pour over the meat slices, and heat in a moderate oven for twenty minutes. Serve with mashed potatoes.

Yorkshire Bald Head Pudding

Prepare a suet crust by mixing eight ounces flour with four ounces finely chopped beef suet and a teaspoon of salt. Mix to a stiff dough with cold water. Roll out two-thirds of the dough to line a large greased pudding basin, leaving enough to make a lid. Put to one side.

Chop one and a half pounds shoulder steak into neat pieces, and roll them in seasoned flour. Trim and slice three-quarters of a pound beast (ox) kidney, and chop up a large onion. Put all into the lined basin, and cover with water or good stock. Dampen the edges of the prepared lid, and seal it down, pressing the joins firmly together. Stand the basin, first covered with greased paper and a well-tied pudding cloth, in a pan of simmering water, and boil gently for four hours. Check from time to time to see that the water level stays just below the rim of the basin and does not boil dry. Turn out on to a warmed dish, deep enough to contain the gravy when the pudding is cut open.

Stand Pie

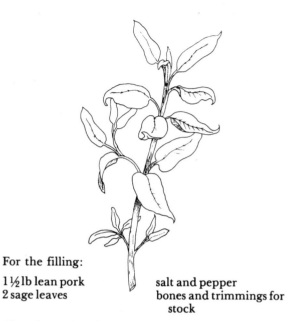

For the pastry:

12oz flour	½ teaspoon salt
5oz lard	¼ pint milk and water

Rub 1 ounce lard into the flour. Put the remainder of the lard and the milk and water into a pan and bring to the boil. Mix with the flour and knead well with the hand. While the dough is still warm, it must be quickly made into a pie case before it cools and cracks. A cylindrical wooden pie mould will help to give a good shape, but a large warmed jam jar will suffice. Divide the dough in half, then cut one piece in half again. Roll these out to make circles for the base and the lid. Stand the pie mould or jar on one, and use the remaining half of the pastry to form the sides. Seal all the joins by damping the pastry and pressing firmly with the fingers, Lift out the mould, and the pie is ready to be filled.

For the filling:

1½lb lean pork	salt and pepper
2 sage leaves	bones and trimmings for stock

Chop the pork and sage leaves finely, season well and pack into the pie case. Dampen the edges of the lid, cover the meat and pinch the edges firmly to seal. Cut a small hole in the top of the pie to let out the steam, brush with beaten egg and bake for an hour and a half in a moderate oven. While the pie cooks, simmer the bones and trimmings in a little water to make a thick jellied stock. This is to be poured into the steam hole before the pie cools and sets.

Pan Pie

A lovely old-fashioned dish, originally made in a large pan over an open fire in the kitchen. Meat, onions, carrots, turnips and plenty of potatoes were cut up and simmered in a heavy pan with water or stock to cover them, seasoned with salt and pepper. There was no crust, and the end result was almost like a thick soup, to be eaten with oatcake or bread. When times were hard there would be hardly any meat in Pan Pie, but the addition of a large marrow-bone made it a flavoursome and satisfying stew.

Yorkshire Squab Pie

8oz lean pork	a cupful of good stock
1 large apple	salt and pepper
2 onions	a little sage
1 large potato	pastry to cover

Slice the onions, apple and potato, and cut the meat into small pieces. Arrange them in layers in a greased pie dish, seasoning with the salt, pepper and sage. Pour over the stock, cover with a thick pastry crust and bake in the oven for one and a half hours, hot at first, then at a moderate heat, when the pastry is crisp.

Oxtail Brawn

Put a jointed ox tail in a heavy stewpot together with an onion stuck with six cloves. Add salt and pepper and just enough water to cover. Stew very gently in the oven for six hours, or until the meat is tender and the bones can be easily removed. Take out the onion, chop the meat and pack it into a mould or basin. Pour over enough of the thick jellied stock to cover the air spaces, put a weighted plate on top and leave in a cold place till set. Remove from the mould and serve cut into slices.

Potted Beef

Put a pound of good stewing or shin beef in a stew pot with a cupful of water, salt, pepper and a little mace. Stew gently until tender in a very low oven. Then put the meat through a mincer twice and stir in a good knob of melted butter. Add more seasoning if necessary, and pack into pots, sealing the tops with a layer of melted butter. Serve spread on bread or toast.

At about the feast of Martinmas on 11 November, beasts were killed before the winter, and the meat salted or cured. Offal and blood had to be used straight away, nothing was wasted, and the following recipes would be useful at this time.

Stuffed Hearts

2 sheep's hearts	1oz chopped parsley
1oz chopped suet	a pinch of thyme
3oz breadcrumbs	salt and pepper
1 egg	teaspoon lemon juice

Wash the hearts through with running water and trim off any loose flaps. Make the stuffing by combining the breadcrumbs, chopped suet, herbs and seasoning, and bind with the egg and lemon juice. Stuff the cavities of the hearts and bake them in an open dish until they are tender, at least an hour in a moderate oven. Baste them from time to time with dripping, and serve with gravy and mashed potatoes.

Black Pudding

1 quart blood	1 plain loaf
1 quart old milk	1 oatcake, crumbled
3lb onions	1oz pork dripping
½lb rice	salt, pepper, sage,
½lb oatmeal	and thyme

Peel, slice and boil the onions. Boil the rice and grate the loaf into crumbs. Put all the ingredients except the blood and the dripping into a large bowl, mix well and taste to see that it is well seasoned. Stir in the blood; the mixture should be very thin, but will become firm when cooked. Melt the dripping in a large shallow meat tin and pour in the black pudding mixture. Bake in a slow oven for at least two hours.

Savoury Liver

Half a pig's liver and the tongue and the heart, and also some leaf fat. Mince them all or cut into very small pieces. Chop the same bulk in onions, add pepper and salt and enough water to barely cover. Bake in a slow oven for four hours.

Stewed Tripe and Savoury Dumplings

1½ lb tripe	a small pinch each of
2 onions	marjoram and ginger
(or 1 onion and 1 leek)	salt and pepper
2 carrots	1 oz butter
1 pint light stock	1 oz flour
1 tablespoon parsley	

Peel and slice the vegetables, cut the tripe into thin strips. Simmer them gently in the light stock together with the herbs and seasoning until all are tender (about an hour). Strain off the liquid, and add it to the butter and flour, cooked together gently in a separate pan. Stir until the sauce is thickened, then pour back over the tripe and vegetables. Serve hot with the following dumplings.

Savoury Dumplings

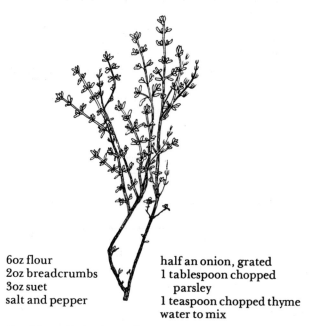

6 oz flour	half an onion, grated
2 oz breadcrumbs	1 tablespoon chopped
3 oz suet	parsley
salt and pepper	1 teaspoon chopped thyme
	water to mix

Combine all the ingredients and mix with just enough water to make a stiff dough. Divide to make small balls and drop into a pan of briskly boiling water. Cook for half an hour.

Haselet

1lb lean beef steak	1 egg
½lb lean ham	salt and pepper
4oz breadcrumbs	

Mince the beef and the ham and mix in the breadcrumbs, salt and pepper. Beat the egg and add to the mixture, forming a stiff paste. Roll in a pudding cloth, tie firmly and boil for 1½ hours. Serve cold in thick slices or fried for breakfast.

To Roast a Grouse

Grouse are plentiful on the moors around Haworth, and their harsh cry of 'Go back, go back' is a familiar sound. This recipe is best for young tender birds; older ones should be given longer slower cooking.

Take one or two brace of grouse, together with a fat rasher of bacon and a piece of toast for each bird. Pluck, draw and wipe the birds, remove their heads and truss them like fowls. Work some lemon juice, pepper and salt into a little butter, and place a piece into each bird's body. Wrap each one in a rasher of fat bacon, and roast in a hot oven for thirty-five minutes, basting often. Then remove the bacon, dredge the birds with flour and put them back in the oven until brown. While the birds are cooking, boil their livers until tender, then pound them in a mortar with a little salt and pepper. Spread this paste on pieces of toast, one for each bird to sit upon. Let them brown for a few minutes more, then serve with bread sauce, watercress, chipped potatoes, and a good brown gravy.

Grouse Pie

A brace of grouse	pinch of salt
8oz lean beef steak	pinch of cayenne pepper
6 rashers bacon	2 teaspoons chopped parsley
2 eggs, hard boiled	8oz flaky pastry

Wash the grouse through with running water, then put them in a pan with just enough water to cover, and simmer for thirty minutes. Remove the grouse, and slice as much meat as possible from the bones. Return the bones to the stock pan and continue to simmer down to make a good gravy.

Grease a pie dish and layer it with the thinly-sliced steak, bacon rashers and grouse meat; with the sliced hard boiled eggs in the centre. Season well and sprinkle with parsley on each layer. Pour over the reduced gravy (about half a pint) and cover with pastry. Bake for an hour and a half in a moderate oven, and serve hot or cold, with Rowan Jelly.

Boiled Fowl

First pluck and clean the fowl. Stuff it with the following forcemeat, tie it up securely and boil it gently for two and a half to three hours. The sauce should be poured over the fowl before serving.

Forcemeat:

3oz breadcrumbs	1 teaspoon thyme
2oz chopped suet	1 egg
1oz chopped parsley	salt and pepper

Mix all together thoroughly and stuff the cavity of the fowl.

Sauce:

2oz butter	½ pint milk
2oz flour	½ pint stock
	salt and pepper

Melt the butter, stir in the flour and let them cook gently for two minutes. Gradually pour over the warmed milk and the stock, stirring all the time until the sauce is thick. Season to taste with salt and pepper.

14

Roast Pigeon

2 young pigeons	1oz butter
2 fat rashers bacon	salt and pepper
2oz breadcrumbs	

Wipe the pigeons inside and out, soften the butter with a wooden spoon, work in the breadcrumbs and seasoning, and roll into two neat balls. Place one inside each bird, and wrap a rasher of bacon round each one. Roast in a hot oven for half an hour, basting with a little butter or dripping. Dip two pieces of toast into the juices in the pan, and serve the pigeons upon these, together with gravy and bread sauce.

Stewed Pigeon

Older birds are better stewed than roasted; put two or three in a large pan with sliced root vegetables and sufficient water or light stock to cover. Bring slowly to the boil; skim the top, and simmer for half an hour, or more if the birds are tough. Serve with mashed potatoes or boiled rice, and a thick parsley and butter sauce. Any left over meat and vegetables can be chopped and added to the stock to make an excellent soup.

Roast Goose

A roast stuffed goose is traditionally served at Michaelmas, together with a good sauce from the early autumn apples. Emily Brontë kept two pet geese, Adelaide and Victoria, in the peat store at the back of Haworth Parsonage; no doubt they felt a little anxious as Michaelmas drew near!

1 young goose, weighing	1½ oz butter
eight to ten pounds	1 oz chopped parsley
6oz breadcrumbs	a pinch of sage
1 large or 2 small onions	salt and pepper
1 egg	

Prepare the goose by removing any pin feathers and wiping thoroughly, inside and out. Chop the goose liver and fry it gently in the butter, then combine it with the breadcrumbs, chopped onions, herbs, salt and pepper.

Bind all together with the beaten egg, adding a little milk if necessary, and stuff the body of the bird. Truss it securely with string, prick the skin all over to allow the fat to trickle out and baste the goose while it cooks. Roast on a rack in a fairly hot oven for three to four hours: twenty minutes to the pound and twenty minutes over. Test with a skewer at the thickest part of the leg to see if the juices run clear. Serve with apple sauce and gravy.

Jugged Hare

Cut the Hare into small pieces, dust them with flour and fry in a little beef dripping until browned on each side. Drain from the fat and place in a large stew jar with a close-fitting lid. Now add about one gill of best Port Wine. Peel a large onion into shreds and fry brown in the same dripping, then cut three quarters of a pound of streaky bacon into small pieces and add these to the contents of the jar, with sufficient stock to well cover. Season with salt and pepper, also a little sage. Stew in a moderate oven for about three hours. Serve in a hot dish with forcemeat balls and red currant jelly.

Forcemeat Balls

Finely mince three ounces of lean raw ham and the same quantity of beef suet. Then add six ounces of bread-crumbs, a teaspooonful of minced parsley, a teaspoonful of chopped thyme, salt, pepper and a little grated lemon rind. Bind all the ingredients together with a beaten egg and mix well. Form the mixture into balls and poach them for twenty minutes in gently simmering water.

Stewed Rabbit

1 rabbit
2 onions
2 carrots
1 large potato

2oz dripping or lard
1oz flour
salt and pepper

Skin and clean the rabbit, cut it into neat joints and put them in a basin. Pour over enough boiling water to cover and leave to stand for a few minutes. Pour off the water and pat the joints dry, then roll them in seasoned flour. Heat the dripping in a thick stewpan, and brown the rabbit joints. Add enough boiling water to cover, and bring back to the boil. Add the vegetables, peeled and sliced, and simmer for two hours. Half an hour before the cooking is done, drop savoury dumplings into the simmering broth, and serve them with the meat and vegetables.

Savoury Dumplings

6oz flour
2oz breadcrumbs
3oz chopped suet
salt and pepper

2 tablespoons chopped
   parsley
a pinch of chopped thyme

Mix all the ingredients well, and add just enough cold water to make a stiff paste. Divide into eight pieces and roll into balls. Cook for half an hour in the broth, keeping the pan covered.

Soups, Vegetables and Savoury Dishes

All the following were said to be particularly good and nourishing for invalids.

Calf's Foot Jelly

Wash two or three calf's feet and cut them into pieces. Cover with cold water and stew gently until the bones fall apart. Strain off the liquid, and leave in a cool place to set. Remove the fat from the top, and put the jelly in a saucepan, leaving any sediment which may have settled on the bottom. Add two tablespoons of brandy, a few strips of lemon peel, and the shells and raw whites of two eggs. Boil all together for fifteen minutes to clarify and then strain through muslin into a mould. Turn out when set.

Sweet Cow Heel Jelly

Parboil a cow heel for twenty minutes, then drain off the water and cut the heel into pieces. Put these in a stewing pot with two pints of milk, a bay leaf, 3oz sugar, and a few strips of lemon peel. Cook gently in the oven for two hours, then strain and add a wineglassful of sherry. This can be served hot, or allowed to cool and set in a mould.

Beef Tea

Take a pound of good lean stewing beef, cut it into small dice and trim off any fat. Put into a pan with a pint of cold water and a little salt, and bring gently to boiling point. Skim off any scum that rises to the surface, and simmer gently for half an hour. Strain the liquid through muslin, and serve hot in a cup. The left over meat may be minced, seasoned and mixed with a little melted butter for potting. Serve spread on toast.

Sheep's Head Broth

Wash the head well in plenty of running water, remove the brains and tongue (these would be used for other dishes) and discard the eyes. Put the head into a large pan together with a chopped onion, and a few sliced root vegetables, such as carrots or turnips. Cover with water and bring to the boil; simmer gently for four hours, skimming off any scum that rises to the surface. Strain off the liquid and pour into a clean pan with a handful of oatmeal, or pearl barley. Season well with salt and pepper and simmer for a further hour.

Oakworth Onion Soup

Peel three large onions and slice them thinly. Melt a large knob of butter in a heavy pan, add the onions and stew them very gently for half an hour over a low heat, stirring occasionally. When they are completely soft, add a quart of good stock and simmer for one hour. Strain the soup and sieve the onions, then return to the pan and season with salt, pepper and a little grated nutmeg. Stir in a quarter of a pint of cream just before serving.

Yorkshire Onion Pasty

3 large onions	8oz flour
salt and pepper	4oz lard
1oz butter	

Peel and slice the onions and parboil them in simmering water until soft, then drain. (The onion water may be used later in soup.) Rub the lard into the flour, keeping it very cool and add just enough cold water to make a stiff paste. Roll out to make a circle, and cover one half with the softened onions. Season with salt and pepper and put little dabs of butter all around. Dampen the edges of the pastry and fold to make a half moon shape. Bake on a baking sheet in a hot oven for fifteen minutes.

Cheese and Onion Pasties

2 onions	8oz flour
2 boiled potatoes	4oz lard
3oz grated cheese	salt and pepper

Peel, slice and parboil the onions until soft, and combine with the grated cheese and chopped potatoes. Rub the lard into the flour and add enough cold water to make a stiff paste. Divide into four, and roll them out into circles. Put a quarter of the cheese, onion and potato mixture in the centre of each and season well. Dampen the edges of the pastry circles and draw together to make pasty shapes, pressing well to seal. Brush with a little milk or egg, and bake in a hot oven until crisp and browned.

Yorkshire Pudding

4oz flour	a good pinch of salt
1 large egg	Meat drippings
½ pint milk	

Put the flour in a large bowl, make a well in the centre to hold the egg and half the milk. Using a wooden spoon, gradually beat the flour into the egg and milk, incorporating it slowly so that there are no lumps. Beat the batter thoroughly for ten minutes; it should sound like the 'clip clop' of a trotting horse as air is beaten into the mixture. Stir in the salt and the rest of the milk and allow the batter to stand for half an hour in a cool place. Meanwhile, heat some drippings in a meat tin until they are smoking hot. Just before pouring the batter into the tin, add a dash of cold water. As it turns to steam it will help the pudding to rise. The secret of the very best Yorkshire Pudding is a tablespoonful of clean snow, rather than water, added just before cooking.
Bake the pudding for about twenty-five minutes at the top of a very hot oven, and serve it straight away with gravy, before the meat.

Pea Soup

½ lb dried green peas	2 tablespoons rice
2 onions	2 tablespoons flour
1 carrot	2 tablespoons oatmeal
1 small turnip	salt and pepper

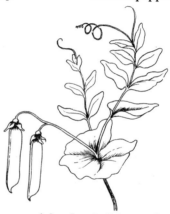

Soak the peas overnight, then boil for one hour in 1½ pints water. Meanwhile slice the onions and fry them until soft in a little butter or bacon fat. Add the carrot and turnip, chopped small, and stir in the flour. Pour over the peas and the boiling water, add the oatmeal, rice, and seasoning and simmer gently until the vegetables are cooked and the rice is soft. A little cream or milk may be stirred in before serving to enrich the soup.

Passion Dock Pudding

This savoury pudding was always eaten during 'Passion Tide' and particularly on Good Friday.

> *Mi love is like the Passion Dock*
> *That grows i' t'summer fog;*
> *An' tho' shoo's but a country lass,*
> *I like mi Sall o' t'Bog.*

(taken from 'Sall o' t'Bog' by William Wright.)

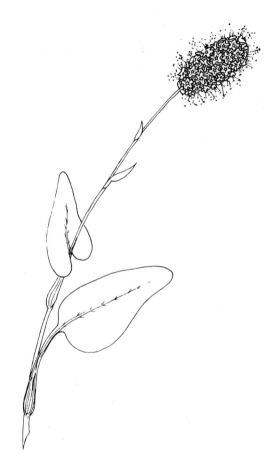

½ lb Passion Dock Leaves   1 egg
½ lb young nettle leaves   a handful of fine oatmeal
1 onion   salt and pepper

Remove any pieces of stalk from the docks and nettles and wash them well in running water. Put them in a pan with a chopped onion and one and a half pints of water; cover and simmer until all are tender. Strain off the liquid, keeping it to one side while the leaves are chopped finely and returned to the pan. Stir in the oatmeal and one egg well beaten, pour over the reserved liquid and bring gently back to the boil, stirring all the time, until thickened. This dish is traditionally served with bacon or ham, and a few of the bacon drippings may be stirred into the pudding to improve the flavour.
(It is important not to confuse the Passion Dock (*Polygonum bistorta*) with the more common Broadleaved Dock (*Rumex Obtusifolius*).

Savoury Bread Pudding

Soak several slices of bread in water or milk and then squeeze very dry. Beat until smooth with a fork. Add three or four par-boiled chopped onions, a teaspoon of chopped sage leaves, a tablespoon of chopped suet and pepper and salt to taste. Bind the mixture with a beaten egg, and turn into a flat dish. Bake in the oven until browned on top. This dish may be eaten hot or cold; it is delicious with roast pork or sausages, or it can be cut into slices and fried in bacon fat for breakfast.

Pease Pudding

½ lb yellow split peas   1 oz bacon drippings
pinch of baking soda   pepper and salt

Soak the yellow split peas overnight, and throw away the soaking water. Put them in a pan with fresh water to cover and a pinch of baking soda. Simmer for two or three hours, adding more water if necessary, until the peas are very soft. Drain them, add the bacon drippings and mash until smooth, seasoning them to taste. Serve with roast pork or ham, piled into a mound with a knob of melted butter on top.

Carlin Peas

Known sometimes as grey or brown peas, these were always eaten on Carlin Sunday, which fell between Mid-Lent and Palm Sunday. They were often served without any charge in public houses.

Steep the peas overnight in plenty of water, then drain and put them in a large pan with enough fresh water to cover. Simmer them gently until cooked, and serve hot with plenty of salt and pepper and a little vinegar sprinkled over. A ham bone buried in the peas as they cook will give a good flavour, or a little bacon fat may be stirred in. Previously-boiled Carlin Peas can be fried in butter or bacon drippings to re-heat them.

Ladies' Cabbage

Take a firm white cabbage, chop it small and boil briskly until tender. Drain off the cabbage water and keep it for soup. Melt a tablespoonful of butter into the cabbage, season it with salt and pepper, then add a well-beaten egg, mixing thoroughly. Put the mixture into a well buttered pie dish and cover with fine breadcrumbs. Bake for half an hour in a hot oven, until the breadcrumbs are browned.

Puddings

An account of the great pudding served to celebrate the opening of the Haworth Railway, on 10 April 1867; written by William Wright, a local poet known as 'Bill o' the Hoylus End'.

Thare wur fifty i' number invited to dine,
All us at hed acted reight loyal to th'line;
Sa I thout that I'd go, for I knew well enuff
'At th' puddings this time wud be made o' th'reight stuff
And noan o' that stuffment that gav th'Keighla band,
Toan awf on it rubbish and tother awf sand.

For twelve stone o' flour (3lbs to a man)
Wur boiled i' oud Bingleechin's kaa lickin pan
Wi gert lumps o' sewet at th'cook hed put in't,
At shane like a ginney just new aat o' th'mint;
Wi nives made a purpos to cut it i' rowls,
An' th' sauce wur i' buckets, an mighty big bowls.

They wur chattin an' tawkin' an' sucking ther spice,
An crackin at dainties thay thout 'at wur nice,
Wal th' oud parson gat up and pulled a long face,
An' mutter'd sum words 'at thay call sayin' th' grace,
But I nivver goam'd that, cos I knew for a fact
It wur nobbut a signal for th'pudding attack.

And I'll tell yo wat, folk, thou yo maint beleeve,
But yo tawk abaat Wibsey folk heytin horse beef,
Yo sud a seen Locker tanners brandishin' thair nives,
An' choppin and cuttin thair wallopin shives,
An' all on em shaating that liked th'pudding th'best,
For nowt wur like th'pudding for standin the test.

According to Bill o'th Hoylus End, this splendid pudding was served in the Black Bull to the accompaniment of lively loud music from the Spring Head Band.

Steamed Puddings

Mix together two tablespoons each of flour, shredded suet, breadcrumbs, and sugar, together with a good pinch of salt and a teaspoon of baking powder. For Lemon Pudding, add the grated rind and juice of one lemon. For Fruit Pudding, two tablespoons each of currants and sultanas. For Fig Pudding, four tablespoons of chopped figs.

Mix the pudding with a well-beaten egg and half a breakfast cup of milk. Turn it into a greased basin and steam for two hours.

High Church Pudding

1 teacup flour	2 tablespoons sugar
1 teacup fine breadcrumbs	2 tablespoons jam
1 teacup shredded suet	½ teaspoon carbonate of
1 egg	soda
	½ teacup milk

Mix the flour and the suet, add the breadcrumbs, the sugar and the carbonate of soda. Mix well, then stir in the jam, the beaten egg and the milk. Steam for three hours in a pudding basin.

Boiled Lemon Pudding

2oz flour	1 egg
2oz breadcrumbs (white)	1 lemon
2oz suet	1 teaspoon baking powder
2oz sugar	a little milk

Grate the lemon and extract the juice. Mix all the dry ingredients well, then add the lemon juice, beaten egg and enough milk to moisten. Turn into a pudding basin, tie greaseproof paper over the top and steam for two hours. Serve with lemon sauce.

Ginger Sponge Pudding

8oz flour	2 teaspoons ground ginger
5oz soft brown sugar	pinch cinnamon
2oz butter	1 teaspoon carbonate of soda
3 tablespoons treacle	⅓ pint milk
1 egg	

Melt the butter, treacle and sugar in a large pan. Stir in the flour, ginger, cinnamon, carbonate of soda and milk and mix well. Beat the egg, and add it last of all for a glossy crust. Pour the batter into a large flat oven tin and bake for one hour, not too hot. Serve hot with custard, or cold with stewed rhubarb.

Gooseberry Sponge Pudding

1lb gooseberries	3 tablespoons milk
6oz sugar	4oz flour
2oz butter	a pinch of salt
1 egg	½ teaspoon baking powder

Top and tail the gooseberries, butter a pudding basin and put the gooseberries in the bottom with half the sugar sprinkled over. Beat the remaining sugar with the butter, add the egg and beat well. Stir in the flour, baking powder, salt and milk and mix thoroughly. Pour the mixture over the fruit in the pudding basin, tie a buttered paper over the top, and steam for one and a half hours. Serve with thick custard.

Bread and Butter Pudding

4 slices bread and butter	1 egg
3oz raisins	½ oz candied peel
1oz sugar	pinch of salt
½ pint milk	

Cut the buttered bread into neat triangles, and arrange them in a buttered pie dish, with the raisins and chopped peel scattered between the slices. Beat the egg with the milk and the salt, and pour over the bread, then sprinkle the sugar on the top. Allow the pudding to stand and soak for an hour and then bake it gently in a moderate oven until set.

Mother Eve's Pudding

If you want a good pudding, to teach you I'm willing;
Take two pennyworth of eggs, when twelve for a shilling;
And of the same fruit that Eve had once chosen;
Well pared and well chopped, at least half a dozen.
Six ounces of bread (let your maid eat the crust)
The crumbs must be grated as fine as the dust.
Six ounces of currants from the stone you must sort,
Lest they break out your teeth, and spoil all your sport.
Six ounces of sugar won't make it too sweet;
Some salt and some nutmeg will make it complete.
Three hours let it boil, without hurry or flutter,
And then serve it hot without sugar or butter

While peeling the apples for the pudding, young cooks may have followed the old custom often associated with the feast of St Simon and St Jude on 28 October:
'Pare a whole apple so that the peeling remains in one long piece. Hold it in your right hand, turn three times round and throw the peel over your left shoulder on to the floor. It will form the initial letter of your future husband's name. If the peel breaks, you will never marry.'

Marguerite Pudding

4oz flour	½ teacup milk
2oz butter	1 teaspoon baking powder
2oz sugar	2 tablespoons jam
1 egg, well beaten	

Rub the butter into the flour, stir in the sugar, baking powder, beaten egg and milk. Line a pudding basin with the jam, pour the mixture over and cover firmly with buttered paper. Steam for one hour and serve with a little cream.

This recipe came from Nurse Hill, who was a midwife in Haworth about fifty years ago. She 'lived in' for a month when a new baby arrived, so presumably her recipes found their way into many family books.

Roly-Poly Pudding

6oz flour	pinch of salt
2oz breadcrumbs	2oz currants or sultanas
2½ oz suet	6oz light treacle
½ teaspoon baking powder	a little lemon juice

Mix the flour, salt, breadcrumbs, suet and baking powder, and add just enough water to make a stiff dough. Knead it well, and roll out on a floured board to make an oblong shape. Warm the treacle and spread it over the suet paste, not quite to the edges. Scatter the fruit over the top, and sprinkle with a little lemon juice. Dampen the edges of the oblong, and roll it up like a bolster, pressing well to seal. Wrap the pudding in several layers of buttered greaseproof paper, tying the ends firmly. Steam for two to three hours, unwrap the pudding on a warm dish and serve cut into slices.

Christmas Pudding

The best time to make Christmas Puddings is in October, so that they can mature for two months before they are eaten. Store them in a cool dark place until December, and then re-steam them for at least an hour. Small favours or well-scrubbed coins can be eased into the pudding with a knifepoint before the final steaming.

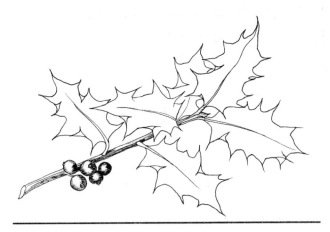

6oz flour
6oz fine breadcrumbs
7oz chopped suet
9oz brown sugar
9oz seeded raisins
9oz currants
3oz mixed peel
wineglass rum or brandy
a little milk

one grated apple
3 eggs, beaten
1 lemon (juice and grated rind)
1 tablespoon ground almonds
1 dessertspoon warm treacle
¼ teaspoon mixed spice
¾ teaspoon carbonate of soda, dissolved in a little water

Wash the fruit and let it stand in a bowl overnight with the spirit and the lemon juice poured over. Then add all the other ingredients, stirring well after each addition and mixing thoroughly. Prepare some pudding basins by lining them with buttered paper, fill with the mixture and tie more buttered paper and pudding cloths over the top, tying down firmly. Steam them in a large saucepan for six hours, taking care that they do not boil dry.
Serve with rum sauce (a sweet white sauce flavoured with a good dash of rum).

Plum Pudding

8oz flour
8oz breadcrumbs
8oz suet
8oz sugar
1 egg
1 gill stout

8oz raisins
8oz currants
½ teaspoon nutmeg
½ teaspoon mixed spice
3 teaspoons baking powder
milk to mix

Chop the suet finely and mix thoroughly with the flour, breadcrumbs and sugar. Stir in the dried fruit, spices and baking powder. Beat the egg, and add it to the pudding mixture together with the stout and a little milk. Steam in a pudding basin for six hours and serve with a sweet white sauce.

Fairy Pudding

The Brontë's servant, Tabby, was old enough to remember the days when fairies lived in the bottom of the valley at Haworth, and had known people who saw them by the beck by moonlight. Alas, the coming of the noisy woollen mills drove them away, but perhaps this pudding served as a reminder. It was only made on special occasions.

Put the juice of two lemons, two breakfast cups of water, and two teacups of sugar into a saucepan, reserving just enough water to smooth down three tablespoonsful of cornflour. Bring the ingredients in the saucepan to a boil, and add carefully to the slaked cornflour, stirring constantly. Return to the heat until the cornflour is thoroughly cooked and the mixture has thickened. Remove from the fire and cool. Whip the whites of four eggs stiffly and mix them with the cooled cornflour mixture. Pour into a mould and leave in a cool place overnight to set. Make the following sauce to serve with the mould:

Mix two teaspoons cornflour with 2 cupfuls milk and 2 ounces sugar. Cook them gently in a saucepan until thickened. Add the four beaten egg yolks, stirring all the time, together with a few drops of vanilla essence. Cook in a double saucepan over hot water until the sauce is smooth and thick. Cool and then serve poured over the pudding.

Fig Pudding

Figs were often used in early spring, when there was little fresh fruit to be had, and were especially associated with Palm Sunday.

8oz figs	4oz sugar
4oz flour	1 egg
4oz breadcrumbs	½ teacup milk
4oz suet	1 teaspoon grated nutmeg

Chop the figs into small pieces and the suet finely. Mix the breadcrumbs, flour, nutmeg, and suet, then add the figs and the sugar. Finally stir in the beaten egg and the milk. Steam in a pudding basin for at least three hours and serve hot.

Collop Monday
Pancake Tuesday
Ash Wednesday
Winking Thursday

Kissing Friday
Mucky Saturday
Clean Sunday

This is the week which marks the beginning of Lent. Most people are familiar with the making and tossing of pancakes on Shrove Tuesday, but Collops are not so widely known. They are round flat pieces of bacon, ham or even potato, dipped in batter and fried in hot fat. Winking Thursday is also known as 'Fritter Thursday', when the following recipe is used.

Fritters

4oz flour
1 egg
1 gill each of milk and water
  mixed
1 oz each currants and
  raisins, or 2 sliced apples

pinch of allspice
pinch of salt
½ teaspoon baking powder
1 tablespoon melted butter

Sift the flour and salt into a bowl and gradually beat in the egg and half the liquid. Beat well, and lastly stir in the remaining liquid, together with the melted butter and the baking powder. Add the dried fruit, or else use the mixture to coat the slices of apple. Fry quickly in deep hot fat until crisp and golden, then serve straight away, sprinkled with sugar.

Brown Betty

2lbs cooking apples, peeled
  and sliced
8oz old bread

6oz brown sugar
cinnamon to taste
3oz butter

Dry out the bread in a low oven until crisp, then crush or roll to fine crumbs. Butter a deep pie dish and sprinkle the bottom and sides with the crumbs. Put a layer of apples in the dish, cover with sugar, cinnamon and more breadcrumbs, and so on until the dish is full, ending with a layer of breadcrumbs. Put small pieces of butter all over the top, then bake in a moderate oven until the apples are soft and the top is well browned.

Ground Rice Tarts

4oz sugar
4oz butter
2 eggs

4oz ground rice
shortcrust pastry

Line some small tart cases or patty tins with shortcrust pastry. Beat the sugar with the butter until they are light and fluffy, then beat in the eggs separately. Add the ground rice and mix well. Fill the pastry cases with the mixture and bake them in a hot oven for about twenty or thirty minutes until they are risen and light brown.

Stanbury Pasty

The village of Stanbury lies a mile or so west of Haworth, and from here comes this recipe for a rich sweet pasty; a teatime treat.

8oz flour	1 teaspoon baking powder
4oz butter	a little milk to mix
3oz sugar	jam for the filling
1 large egg	

Rub the butter into the sifted flour and baking powder, stir in the sugar, the beaten egg and enough milk to make a firm light dough. Divide the dough into four, and roll each piece out on a floured board to a circle, about six to eight inches across. Spread two of them with jam, not quite to the edges, and cover with the remaining two circles. Seal round the edges with the tip of a fork, pressed flat against the pastry. Bake the pasties in a hot oven for twenty minutes, and serve cold, cut into quarters.

Treacle Tart

½ lb shortcrust pastry	1 lemon
6oz breadcrumbs	4 tablespoons light treacle

Line a pie dish with the pastry, grate the bread to fine crumbs, and grate the rind from the lemon. Warm the treacle and lemon juice in a pan, and stir in the breadcrumbs and lemon rind. Fill the pie with the mixture and bake in a hot oven for half an hour.

Bilberry Pie

The beautiful moors near Haworth provide a free harvest of bilberries for pies and tarts in summer. Plenty of patience and nimble fingers are needed to gather the tiny blue-black berries, but their unique smoky flavour makes the effort worthwhile.

Line a shallow dish or pie-plate with shortcrust pastry, fill with bilberries and dredge with sugar. A little lemon juice may be sprinkled over, but not too much because the berries are extremely juicy. Cover them with a pastry top, dampen and seal the edges, and make one or two scissor-snips in the centre to allow steam to escape. Bake in a quick oven until the pastry is crisp. Serve hot with custard or cold with cream.

Mint Pasty

½ cupful chopped mint
2oz currants
2oz raisins
2oz sugar

1 large apple
tablespoon lemon juice
½ lb shortcrust pastry

Peel, core and finely chop the apple. Mix it with the sugar, lemon juice, mint and dried fruit. Roll out the pastry to a large circle, and spread the filling on one half, leaving a rim of pastry for sealing. Dampen the edges of the circle, and fold over the unfilled half, to make a semi-circular pasty. Seal the edges, brush the top with milk, and bake on an oven sheet for twenty to thirty minutes in a hot oven. Serve hot or cold.

The filling can be divided between several small pastry circles to make individual pasties if preferred.

30

Beestings

The first milk from a newly-calved cow is called 'Beestings' and it can be used to enrich a variety of dishes. A cupful may be stirred into Rice Pudding, making it creamy and yellow; or it can be used in place of eggs in Yorkshire Puddings. The most usual way of serving Beestings is baked in a deep pastry case, sweetened with sugar and a few currants. Cook gently until firm and set, then cool and serve in slices with cream.

Frumenty

This old Yorkshire dish, a kind of porridge, was served for supper on Christmas Eve, but the cooking began several days before.

Take four ounces of whole wheat (sometimes known as 'pearled wheat') and cook it as slowly as possible in gently simmering water until it becomes soft and jellied. This process originally took three days in the coolest part of the kitchen range, stirring from time to time, and adding more water or milk if necessary. Before serving, the Frumenty was sweetened with sugar or honey, and spiced with a little nutmeg or cinnamon. Currants or raisins can be added and it should be served with hot new milk or a little cream.

Junket

2 pints new milk
2oz sugar
grated nutmeg

2 drops vanilla essence
2 teaspoons rennet

Heat the milk very gently to just below blood heat, and stir in the sugar and vanilla essence. When the sugar is dissolved, stir in the rennet, and leave the junket to set in a warm place. Chill before serving, and sprinkle a little grated nutmeg on the top.

Mincemeat

½lb finely chopped beef suet
½lb stoned raisins
½lb currants
½lb sultanas
¼lb mixed peel
½lb moist sugar

1lb finely chopped apple
the grated rind and juice
of one lemon
1 heaped teaspoon mixed
spice
1 gill brandy

Thoroughly mix all the ingredients, pack into jars and store in a cool dry place. The mincemeat will keep for one year if stirred occasionally, and should be allowed to stand for two months before using to improve the flavour.

Marrow Tarts

1lb vegetable marrow
1lb lump sugar
3oz butter

the juice and grated rind
of two lemons
shortcrust pastry

Remove the skin and seeds from the marrow, cut it into small pieces and steam it until tender. Drain and mash well with a fork, then return it to the pan with the sugar, butter, lemon juice and grated rind. Simmer gently, stirring all the time until the mixture is smooth and thick. Allow it to cool and use it as a filling for pastry tarts with a lattice of pastry to decorate the tops.

This filling keeps well if covered and put in a cool place.

Yorkshire Curd Tarts

It was the custom to eat these at sheep-shearing time.

½ lb shortcrust pastry
8oz curds
3oz butter
2oz sugar

2 eggs, separated
½ teaspoon grated nutmeg
the grated peel of one lemon
2oz currants or sultanas

Beat the butter with the sugar, then add the curds and the egg yolks and mix well. Stir in the peel, the nutmeg and the dried fruit. Finally fold in the beaten egg whites. Use the pastry to line several small patty pans, and fill with the mixture.

Bake in a moderate oven for half an hour.

Baked Custard Tart

Line a deep pie dish with short crust pastry, and fill with the following mixture:

1 pint of milk, slightly
  warmed
4 small, or 3 large eggs

1 heaped tablespoon sugar
a little grated nutmeg

Dissolve the sugar in the warmed milk, and beat the eggs thoroughly. Beat in the warm milk, taking care that it is not too hot, or it will curdle the eggs. Pour into the pastry case and grate some nutmeg over the top. Bake for thirty or forty minutes, hot at first, then at a lower heat, until the custard is set and the pastry firm. Allow to cool, and serve cut in slices.

Cakes, Buns and Biscuits

Christmas Cake

1lb flour
12oz butter
12oz moist sugar
6 eggs
2 tablespoons treacle
2 tablespoons rum
pinch of salt
1lb currants

1lb sultanas
4oz raisins
2oz mixed peel
4oz ground almonds
½ teaspoon mixed spice
½ teaspoon ground nutmeg
2 teaspoons baking powder

Beat the butter and sugar to a cream. Add the eggs alternately with tablespoons of sifted flour, beating well after each addition. Fold in the rest of the flour, the salt, mixed spice and nutmeg. Stir in the fruit, rum and treacle, together with the almonds and mixed peel. Bake in a double lined and greased ten-inch cake tin for six hours in a slow oven.

Pepper Cake

A well-spiced treacle cake, traditionally given to carol singers at Christmas time.

1½lb flour
8oz dark sugar
1½lb black treacle
8oz butter
4 large eggs

1oz powdered cloves
1 teaspoon bicarbonate of soda
a little milk

Rub the butter into the flour, stir in the cloves and the sugar, then add the warmed treacle and the eggs, well beaten. Dissolve the bicarbonate of soda in about half a teacup of milk and add last. Mix well, adding a little more milk if necessary. Bake in a moderate oven for one and a half hours.

Bride Cake

1lb best butter	1lb currants
1lb sugar	8oz sultanas
8 eggs	8oz raisins
1lb flour	4oz peel (orange & lemon)
2 teaspoons baking powder	4oz ground almonds
pinch of salt	wineglass of brandy

Beat the butter until pale, add the sugar and beat again. Add the eggs, one at a time, and fold in the flour, sifted with the salt and baking powder. Mix in the fruit, peel and ground almonds, and stir in the brandy. A little milk may be added if the mixture is too dry. Bake in a slow oven for three or four hours, test with a skewer to see if it is done. Keep in a tin for four weeks before covering with almond paste and sugar icing.

Icing for Cakes

Allow one pound of sugar to the whites of four eggs. The sugar to be put into a saucepan with just enough water to moisten it, then let it boil to a thick syrup. Beat the egg whites to a stiff froth, and then pour the syrup on to the froth in a steady stream, beating all the time. Keep beating until the ingredients are cooled, and spread over the cake.

Bible Cake

Also known as 'Scripture Cake', this was especially popular for chapel outings and teas, and a good test of Bible knowledge*.

1 ½lb Judges V, v 25 (Last Clause)
2 ½lb Jeremiah VI, v 20
3 1 tablespoon 1 Samuel XIV, v 25
4 3 of Jeremiah XVII, v 11
5 ½lb 1 Samuel XXX, v 12
6 ½lb Nahum III, v 12 (chopped)
7 2oz Numbers XVII, v8 (blanched and chopped)
8 1lb 1 Kings IV, v 22
9 Season to taste with II Chronicles IX, v 9
10 A pinch of Leviticus II, v 13
11 1 teaspoon of Amos IV, v 5
12 3 tablespoons of Judges IV, v 19

Beat numbers 1, 2, and 3 to a cream, add 4, one at a time, still beating; then 5, 6, 7 and beat again; add 8, 9, 10 and 11, having previously mixed them, then add number 12.
If you have followed Solomon's advice (Proverbs XXIII v14), then your cake will be good. Bake it in a moderate oven for one and a half hours.

(* the answers are on page 37)

Farmhouse Cake

10oz flour	1lb currants
6oz butter	8oz sultanas or raisins
6oz moist sugar	4oz chopped almonds
3 eggs	2 tablespoons light treacle
a wineglass of rum	1 teaspoon baking powder
a little milk	a pinch of mixed spice

Beat the butter with the sugar and then beat in the eggs, one by one. Stir in the treacle, fruit, nuts, spice, and the flour, sifted with the baking powder. Add the rum and just enough milk to make the mixture soft but not too loose. Bake in a well-lined cake tin for three hours in a cool oven. This cake keeps well and is excellent with cheese.

Slab Cake

8oz butter	4oz sultanas
8oz sugar	1 tablespoon ground almonds
8oz flour	2oz ground rice
4 eggs	2 teaspoons baking powder
4oz currants	

Beat the butter and sugar to a cream, beat in the eggs, one at a time, and stir in the flour, ground almonds, ground rice, baking powder and the fruit. Bake in a moderate oven for an hour and a half. A lovely moist cake for eating straight away.

Feather Cake

1lb flour	½ pint milk
3oz butter	1 teaspoon baking powder
12oz sugar	1 teaspoon carbonate of soda
2 eggs	1 teaspoon cream of tartar

Rub the butter into the flour, add the baking powder, cream of tartar and the sugar. Dissolve the carbonate of soda in the warmed milk, beat the eggs, and add both to the cake mixture.
Turn quickly into a large square tin or two small ones, and bake in a moderate oven for thirty to forty minutes. Cool on a rack and serve cut into squares. A delicious light cake.

Simnel Cake

Until the end of the nineteenth century, it was the custom for young girls in service as maids in large houses, to visit their homes on Mid-Lent Sunday. A Simnel Cake was baked and taken home as a gift for the family on this happy day.

8oz flour	2oz chopped candied lemon
8oz sugar	peel
8oz currants	4 eggs
6oz butter	a good pinch of mixed spice
	a pinch of salt

For the almond icing:
5oz ground almonds	1 egg
5oz sugar	

First make the almond icing by mixing thoroughly together the ground almonds, sugar and the egg. Divide into two and put on one side.

For the cake, cream together the butter and the sugar and beat in the eggs, one at a time, adding a tablespoonful of flour alternately with the eggs. Stir in the currants, the lemon peel, the salt and the spice, and fold in the remaining flour. Put half the cake mixture into a well-greased and lined nine-inch cake tin. Roll out half of the almond paste to a quarter-inch thick circle, and place it gently over the cake mixture. Cover with the rest of the mixture. Bake for two and a half hours in a moderate oven. As it cooks, roll out the remaining almond icing to make a second circle. Press this firmly on to the cake, fifteen minutes before it is done.

Plum Cake

12oz flour	8oz Valencia raisins
4oz ground almonds	8oz currants
4 eggs	1oz lemon peel
8oz butter	2 tablespoons lemon juice
8oz sugar	2 tablespoons brandy
8oz sultanas	2 teaspoons baking powder

Beat the butter until pale and soft, then beat in the sugar. Add the eggs singly, beating after each addition. Stir in the flour, ground almonds, baking powder, sultanas, raisins, currants, peel, lemon juice and brandy. Bake for two to three hours in a moderate oven, test with a skewer to see if it is ready.

This cake improves if it is kept for a while before cutting.

Seed Cake

8oz flour
4oz butter
4oz sugar
2 eggs

2 teaspoons caraway seeds
1 teaspoon baking powder
a little milk

Beat the butter with the sugar until pale and fluffy then beat in the eggs one at a time and fold in the flour, sifted with the baking powder. Add the caraway seeds and mix well, adding enough milk to make a fairly soft consistency. Bake in a moderate oven for about thirty minutes.

St. George's Hall Cake

1lb flour
6oz butter
6oz sugar
6oz currants

2oz candied peel
4 eggs
2 teaspoons baking powder

Sift the flour into a bowl with the baking powder. Rub in the butter, then stir in the sugar, currants and peel. Beat the eggs and add to the mixture. If the consistency is a little dry, add some milk. Bake in a moderate oven for 1½ hours.

Bible Cake Ingredients

For recipe on page 34

1   Butter
2   Sugar
3   Honey
4   Eggs
5   Raisins

6   Figs (chopped)
7   Almonds
    (blanched and chopped)
8   Flour
9   Spice (ground)

10   Salt
11   Leaven (baking powder)
12   Milk

And the advice of Solomon is to beat it well!

Parkin

8oz flour
8oz medium oatmeal
8oz light treacle
4oz moist sugar
4oz butter
4oz sultanas (optional)

1 large egg
2 teaspoons ground ginger
1 teaspoon carbonate of soda
pinch of salt
1 gill milk

Warm the treacle, butter and sugar in a pan until they are melted and smooth, then remove from the fire and stir in the flour, oatmeal and ginger. Dissolve the carbonate of soda in the milk, and beat the egg and add these to the mixture together with a pinch of salt and a handful of sultanas if desired. Pour the soft mixture into a large straight-sided tin and cook for one hour in a moderate oven. Cool and serve cut in squares. This parkin keeps well in an airtight tin.

Gingerbread or 'Moggy'

1lb flour
4oz butter
4oz sugar
8oz treacle

2 eggs
½oz ground ginger
1 teaspoon carbonate of soda
1 gill milk

Sift the flour and the ginger into a bowl. Melt together the butter, sugar and treacle. Beat the eggs. Mix the melted ingredients with the flour, and then add the eggs. Dissolve the carbonate of soda in the milk, and add last. Pour the mixture into a shallow flat tin and bake in a slow oven for an hour and a quarter.

Keeping the Gingerbread in an airtight tin for three days will improve the texture of the cake.

Plain Buns

4oz flour
3oz sugar
2oz butter

1 egg
½ teaspoon carbonate of soda
¼ teaspoon cream of tartar

Beat the butter and sugar to a cream, add the egg and beat well, then fold in the sifted flour and cream of tartar. Dissolve the carbonate of soda in a little milk and stir it in last of all. This recipe will make about a dozen buns. Bake them in a hot oven for fifteen minutes.

Rice Buns

4oz butter	8oz ground rice
4oz sugar	1 teaspoon baking powder
4 eggs	¼ pint milk
4oz flour	

Beat the butter and sugar to a cream, then add the eggs one by one, beating well after each one is added. Stir in the milk and the dry ingredients very lightly, then spoon into bun tins and bake for fifteen minutes in a moderate oven.

Ginger Buns

1½lb flour	1lb syrup
6oz butter or lard	½oz ginger
¾lb sugar	½oz cream of tartar
1 pint milk	½oz bicarbonate of soda

Beat the fat and sugar together, stir in the warmed syrup, then add the flour, ginger and cream of tartar. Dissolve the bicarbonate of soda in the milk and stir it into the mixture. Bake the buns in a moderate oven for about twenty minutes.

Aunt Martha Ann's Raspberry Buns

3oz flour	1 egg
3oz ground rice	1 teaspoon baking powder
2oz sugar	raspberry jam for the filling
2oz butter	

Cream the butter and sugar, beat in the egg, fold in the ground rice and the flour sifted with the baking powder. Divide into small balls, flatten them slightly and place a teaspoon of raspberry jam in the centre of each. Draw together again to seal in the jam, brush with beaten egg, sprinkle with sugar and bake in a fairly hot oven until browned.

Madeline Cakes

2 eggs
2oz sugar
2oz butter

2oz flour
2 drops vanilla flavouring

Beat the eggs in a basin, add the sugar and place over a pan of very hot (not boiling) water and beat until thick. This will take about ten minutes. Meanwhile, stand the butter in a warm place to melt, and add it to the egg mixture together with the flour and vanilla, folding in with a light hand. Bake in small tins for ten or fifteen minutes in a moderate oven.

Queen Cakes

8oz flour
8oz butter
8oz sugar
4 eggs

8oz currants
the grated rind of a lemon
1 teaspoon baking powder

Beat the butter with the sugar until the mixture is fluffy and pale, then beat in the eggs, one at a time. Fold in the sifted flour and baking powder and add the currants and grated lemon rind. Bake in small tins in a fairly quick oven until risen and lightly browned.

Ginger Snaps

1lb flour
8oz sugar
4oz butter
3 tablespoons syrup or
  treacle

1 large teaspoon ground
  ginger
1 teaspoon bicarbonate
  of soda

Melt the syrup, butter and sugar in a large pan, stir in the ginger and the flour and the bicarbonate of soda, dissolved in a very little water. Mix well to a firm paste and allow to cool slightly. Roll out fairly thin on a lightly floured board, and stamp out shapes with a plain biscuit cutter. A split almond may be pressed into the top of each one. Bake them in a moderate oven for twenty-five minutes and let them cool on a wire rack. They will be soft when they leave the oven, but become crisp and brittle as they cool.

Brandy Snaps

4oz flour
4oz brown sugar
4oz golden syrup
4oz butter

1 teaspoon ground ginger
1 teaspoon grated lemon rind
1 teaspoon brandy

Melt the sugar, the butter and the syrup very gently in a pan. Add the ginger and the lemon rind and mix well.

Take the pan off the heat and add the flour, stirring thoroughly. Finally add the brandy. Grease a large baking sheet and drop the mixture in teaspoonsful, about three inches apart. Allow plenty of room for them to spread. Bake in a moderate oven for ten minutes, and as soon as they are done, roll them round the handle of a wooden spoon to make little lacy tubes. They will rapidly become brittle and crisp as they cool. Fill with whipped cream, flavoured with a few drops of brandy.

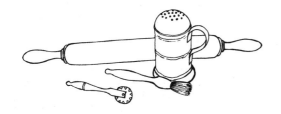

Jumble Biscuits

4oz butter	1 egg
4oz sugar	the grated rind of a lemon,
6oz flour	or, a few drops of essence
	of vanilla

Beat the butter to a cream, add the sugar and beat well and then add the flavouring. Beat in the egg and fold in the flour. Pass through a biscuit forcer to make fancy shapes on a baking sheet. Cook in a moderate oven.

Easter Biscuits

8oz flour	½ teaspoon mixed spice
4oz butter	1 egg
4oz sugar	grated peel and juice of a
2oz currants	lemon
1 teaspoon baking powder	a few drops of brandy

Rub the butter into the flour, add the currants, sugar, baking powder, mixed spice and grated lemon peel. Beat the egg with a dash of brandy, and add to the mixture with just enough lemon juice to make a stiff paste. Roll out very thin and cut into shapes with a round cutter. Bake in a hot oven for fifteen minutes.

Oatmeal Biscuits

8oz wholemeal flour	3oz sugar
8oz oatmeal	1 teaspoon cream of tartar
a good pinch of salt	1 teaspoon carbonate of soda
4oz butter or lard	milk to mix

Rub the butter or lard into the mixed flour, oatmeal and salt. Stir in the sugar, cream of tartar and carbonate of soda and mix well. Add enough milk to make a stiff dough, roll out to ¼-inch thickness and cut into circles with a biscuit cutter. Bake in a slow oven until crisp and lightly browned.

Funeral Biscuits

1lb flour	3 beaten eggs
4oz butter	1 teaspoon caraway seeds
4oz sugar	a pinch of salt

Rub the butter into the flour, stir in the sugar, salt and caraway seeds and mix to a firm dough with the beaten eggs. Roll out thinly on a floured board, cut into shapes and prick with a fork before baking in a hot oven until lightly browned.

Crackneys

1lb flour	¾ oz yeast
6oz lard	4oz currants
2oz butter	a pinch of salt

Crumble the yeast in a little warm water to dissolve, and rub the fat into the flour. Mix together the flour, salt, currants and yeast to make a stiff dough. Leave to stand for half an hour, then roll out on a floured board and cut into circles or squares. Let them rise on a baking sheet for twenty minutes and bake in a hot oven until crisp.

Yorkshire Fat Rascals

These are sometimes known as 'Turf Cakes' and were originally cooked on a bake-stone over an open fire.

8oz flour	1 egg
4oz butter	a pinch of salt
2oz sugar	a little milk
2oz currants	1 teaspoon baking powder

Rub the butter into the flour, stir in the sugar, currants and salt and mix to a light dough with the beaten egg, milk and baking powder. Roll out on a floured board to half an inch thickness, and cut into circles. Bake the cakes on a lightly-greased sheet in a fairly hot oven for fifteen or twenty minutes. Cool and serve them well buttered.

Bread

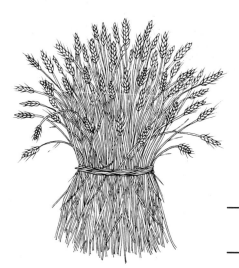
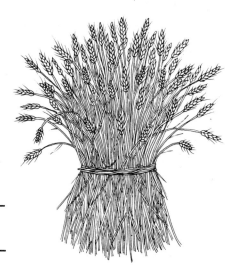

Plain Bread

Emily Brontë was an excellent cook, and made all the bread at Haworth Parsonage when Tabby, the servant, became too old and infirm. She studied German as she kneaded the dough, with a text book propped up before her at the kitchen table; but despite having her attention so divided, the loaves were always light and delicious.

Take three pounds of flour in a large warm bowl, and make a well in the centre. From one and a half pints of warm water, take a teacupful, and crumble an ounce of fresh yeast into it. Pour the dissolved yeast mixture into the well in the flour, sprinkle a little of the flour over the top, then cover the bowl with a cloth and leave it for ten minutes or so to form a 'sponge'. Meanwhile, melt two ounces of lard or butter and mix this into the flour. together with an ounce of salt and the rest of the warm water. Stir thoroughly and then turn the dough out on to a floured board and knead it well, for about ten minutes. Replace the dough in the bowl when it is smooth and springy, cover again with a cloth, and leave it in a warm, draught-free place to rise. Prepare some greased loaf tins and have a good hot oven ready. When the dough has doubled in size, knock it back gently, and divide into several pieces, enough to half fill each tin. Let the dough rise again until it fills the tins, then bake in a hot oven for thirty or forty minutes. The loaves will be done when a knuckle rapped on the bottom of the tin makes a hollow sound. Cool them on a wire rack.

Haverbread

These thin oatcakes were once made and sold throughout Yorkshire; their name is derived from the word 'haver' meaning oats. (A haversack was originally used for the carrying of oats.) Haverbread can be eaten while it is still new and soft, but it was generally hung over a rack or 'flake' to become dry and crisp. A ceiling clothes rack is sometimes still locally known as a 'bread flake'.

Take an ounce of fresh yeast and crumble it into a pint of warmed milk and water, stirring until dissolved. Mix this with a pound of fine oatmeal and a teaspoon of salt. Add enough warmed water to make a batter, and leave the mixture in a warm place for one hour. Heat a large griddle or heavy flat pan and grease it lightly. Stir the oatmeal batter and pour enough of the mixture to make a thin oval on the griddle. Cook until set and leathery, but not browned. If the oatcakes are thick they must be turned and cooked on both sides. When cooked, hang over a rack to dry.

A quarter of the quantity of oatmeal may be replaced with wholemeal flour if preferred. This will help to bind the haverbread and make it easier to handle.

Plain Tea Cakes

1lb flour	1 teaspoon sugar
2oz lard	2 teaspoons salt
½oz yeast	½ pint milk and water

Rub the lard into the flour, warm the milk and water, add the sugar and crumble in the yeast. When dissolved, stir into the flour, add the salt and beat well. Leave in a cool place overnight to rise, or alternatively use an ounce of yeast and rise in a warm place if they are required the same day. Divide the dough into ten pieces, shape them into rounds, flatten with the hands and brush the tops with milk. Put on baking sheets and leave in a warm place for fifteen minutes to rise. Dust the tops with flour, press a floured finger into the centre of each and bake for fifteen or twenty minutes in a hot oven.

Yorkshire Tea Cakes

2lb flour	1 teaspoon salt
4oz sugar	1 pint warm milk
4oz lard or butter	1oz mixed peel
1½oz yeast	1 egg
4oz currants	a pinch of nutmeg

Crumble the yeast in a little of the warm milk, and leave in a warm place until it froths. Sift the flour, salt and nutmeg into a warmed bowl, and stir in the sugar. Beat the egg and melt the butter or lard, then stir both into the flour together with the yeast and the rest of the milk. Add the currants and the peel as you knead the dough lightly, then leave it to rise for twenty minutes, covered with a floured cloth. Divide the dough into flat cakes, four or five ounces each and allow them to rise a little on baking sheets before baking in a hot oven. They should be ready in fifteen minutes, and are delicious split and buttered while still warm.

Yorkshire Half Thicks

These are sometimes known as Oven Bottom Cakes.

2lb strong flour	1 teaspoon sugar
1½oz yeast	½ pint warm milk
6oz lard	½ pint warm water
2 teaspoons salt	

Rub the lard into the flour, dissolve the yeast in half the water and pour it into a well in the centre of the flour to form a sponge. Sprinkle a little of the flour over the top, and when the yeast breaks through, add the rest of the liquid, and the sugar and salt. Knead well, then leave in a warm place to rise. Knock back and divide into twelve or fourteen pieces, and roll them out into flat cakes. Let them rise for twenty minutes on a baking sheet, then bake in a quick oven for twenty minutes. Serve split, toasted and buttered, or with hearty fillings for a packed lunch.

Sad Cakes

1¼lb plain flour	small handful salt
½lb lard	½ pint of milk
2 level dessertspoons baking powder	2oz currants
	2oz sugar

Sift together the flour, salt and baking powder. Rub in the lard, and stir in the milk to make a firm dough. Divide into six round cakes. Make a hole in the cakes with the thumbs and fill with currants and a little sugar. Seal the opening and then flatten the cakes with a rolling pin to about ½ inch thickness, taking care to keep the currants enclosed, or they will burn in the oven. Bake in a hot oven, close to the top, for fifteen minutes.

Suet Cakes

Sometimes known as 'Fatty Cakes' these were eaten for breakfast and tea and are rich and filling. Unlike Sad Cakes, they are made with yeast, and the texture is lighter and spongier.

1lb flour	4oz currants
4oz suet	1oz yeast
4oz lard	milk and water to mix
a good pinch of salt	

Crumble the yeast in a cupful of the milk and water to dissolve. Rub the lard into the flour, and stir in the chopped suet, salt and currants. Add the yeast and enough milk and water to make a dough. Knead thoroughly and divide into eight pieces. Form them into flattened round cakes, and leave to rise on a baking sheet. Bake in a hot oven.

Hot Cross Buns

1lb plain flour	1 egg
1oz butter	½ pint warm milk
1oz lard	¾oz yeast
3oz sugar	1 teaspoon mixed spice
3oz currants	a good pinch of salt
1oz candied peel	

Sift the flour, salt and mixed ground spice into a large warmed bowl. Rub in the fat and add the sugar and the currants. Mix the yeast with a teaspoon of sugar and add half of the warm milk. Make a hollow in the centre of the flour and pour in the yeast mixture. Stir in a little of the flour to make a thin batter. Leave in a warm place for ten minutes. Then mix in the beaten egg and the rest of the warm milk to form a soft dough. Cover it with a cloth and leave it in a warm place until doubled in size. Divide the dough into twelve pieces and knead gently to form buns. Leave them on baking trays in a warm place to rise again and then bake them in a hot oven for ten minutes. Glaze with sugar and milk.

Whitsuntide Buns

Before the establishment of Board Schools in the latter part of the nineteenth century, chapel Sunday Schools were the only means of education for many of the poorer children in Haworth. These children were set to work long hours in the mills from the age of eight; and so their reading, writing and spelling were learnt on Sunday in the chapel schoolroom. The highlight of the Sunday School year came at Whitsuntide, when the children walked through the village in a procession led by a band, and returned to the schoolroom for tea. Home-brewed beer and spicy bread buns were provided for them.

2lb flour
3oz lard
2oz butter
4oz sugar
½ pint milk
½ pint warm water

12oz currants
4oz raisins
1oz grated lemon peel
2½oz yeast
1 teaspoon mixed spice

Dissolve the yeast in a cupful of warm milk and water. Rub the lard and butter into the flour and stir in the sugar, currants, raisins, peel and spice. Add the yeast and the rest of the liquid to make a light dough. Mix thoroughly with the hands and leave to rise for half an hour covered with a cloth. Divide the dough to make round buns—about two dozen—and let them rise again on a baking sheet for twenty minutes or so. Brush the tops with milk and bake them in a hot oven until they rise, shiny and brown.

Potato Griddle Cakes

1 teacup mashed potatoes
1 teacup flour
2 eggs

1½ teacups milk
½ teaspoon salt
2 teaspoons baking powder

Sift the flour, salt and baking powder into a bowl. Beat the eggs, and add them with the milk and mashed potato to the dry ingredients. Mix well to a smooth batter, and bake in tablespoonsful on a hot griddle.

Aunt Ann's Yule Bread

3½lb flour
2oz yeast
8oz raisins
12oz currants
12oz sugar
4oz grated lemon peel

10oz butter or lard
2 eggs
1 nutmeg, grated
1 pint warmed milk
a good pinch of salt

Rub the fat into the flour, make a well in the centre and pour in the yeast, dissolved in half the warm milk. Stir in a little of the flour to make a thin batter, sprinkle more of the flour on top, and leave in a warm place for twenty minutes or so, till a sponge forms and breaks through the flour. Then add the beaten eggs, nutmeg, salt, peel, sugar and the rest of the milk. Mix to a soft dough, and knead well, incorporating the raisins and currants as you do so. Leave to rise for several hours, or overnight in a cool place, covered with a floured cloth. Divide the dough between three or four large loaf tins, well greased inside, and allow the dough to rise and fill the tins. Bake in a hot oven until they sound hollow when rapped on the bottom with a knuckle. Serve sliced and well buttered, with cheese and elderberry wine.

Potato Cakes

It is well worth keeping aside a pound of yeast dough when baking bread, to make these excellent cakes.

8oz mashed potato   4oz flour
1lb yeast dough   4oz lard
1 teaspoon salt

Melt the lard and mix thoroughly with the mashed potato and the salt. Add the yeast dough and sufficient flour to make a firm dough. Knead well for about ten minutes until the dough is smooth and elastic. Divide into eight pieces, shape into balls and then flatten them with rolling pin. They should be about half an inch thick. Leave them to rise on baking sheets for half an hour in a warm place, then bake in a hot oven until risen and brown. Serve split and buttered.

Yorkshire Plum Bread

8oz flour   4oz currants
1oz yeast   4oz sultanas
3oz butter   grated rind of one lemon
2oz sugar   ½ teaspoon cinnamon
1 egg   ½ teaspoon mixed spice
pinch of salt   2 tablespoons milk

Add a dash of hot water to the milk and crumble the yeast into this. Rub the butter into the flour and stir in the sugar, salt, currants, sultanas, lemon peel and spices. Beat the egg and add it to the dry ingredients together with the yeast mixture. Add a little more milk if the mixture is too dry; just enough to make a firm dough. Knead well, divide between two loaf tins and leave to rise for thirty to forty minutes, until the dough fills the tins. Bake in a moderate oven for 1 to 1½ hours. Turn out and cool on a wire rack, serve sliced and buttered.

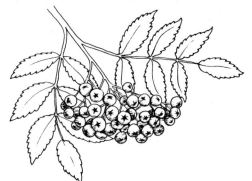

Preserving

Rowan Jelly

Gather sufficient ripe berries from the Rowan, or Mountain Ash tree. These will be at their best in October. Trim the stalks, and put in a pan with a few chopped tart apples to help the set. Cover with water and simmer until all the fruit is completely soft. Strain through a jelly bag, measure the juice and return to a pan with a pound of sugar to each pint of juice. Boil until the setting point is reached, then pot and seal. Rowan jelly should be served with any game bird, and is excellent with roast lamb or mutton.

Crab Apple Jelly

Wipe the crab apples and cut them up roughly. Put them in a pan with just enough water to cover, and bring them to the boil. Simmer to a soft pulp, then strain through a jelly bag or fine muslin. Do not squeeze the pulp, or the jelly will be cloudy. Add a pound of loaf sugar to each quart of juice, bring slowly to the boil, stirring until all the sugar is dissolved. Boil steadily until the setting point is reached; test by leaving a few drops to cool on a saucer to see if they set. Pot and cover in the usual way.

Blackberry Jelly

Cook eight pounds of blackberries in a quart of water until they are soft. Strain through a jelly bag or hair sieve, but do not rub or squeeze the pulp. Measure the juice and return to the pan with three-quarters of a pound of loaf sugar to each pint of juice. Let it boil steadily for thirty or forty minutes keeping it well skimmed. Test a little on a cold saucer to see if it jellies. Pot and seal.

Lemon Cheese

4oz butter	5 eggs
12oz sugar	the juice of 4 lemons

Put the sugar and lemon juice in a large jug or bowl, set over a pan of hot water. Add the butter cut into small pieces, and the eggs, well beaten. Stir constantly over a gentle heat until all are dissolved and the mixture thickens. Do not allow to boil or it will curdle.

Aunt Ellen's Rhubarb Jam

Cut four pounds of rhubarb into small pieces and mix with the grated rind and juice of two lemons. Add five pounds of sugar and leave to stand for twenty-four hours. Then bring to the boil, stirring all the time, and boil steadily for half an hour. This jam should be made during August, and keeps well.

Miss Metcalfe's Egg Plum Jam

Cook seven pounds of egg plums in a pint of water, until they 'fall'. Remove the stones and add seven pounds of sugar. Return to the heat and boil gently for twenty minutes. Pot and seal.

Rhubarb Marmalade

To each pound of rhubarb allow the juice of half a lemon, one pound of sugar, four ounces of chopped blanched almonds, a teaspoon of grated lemon peel and a stick of bruised ginger. Cut the rhubarb into half-inch pieces and place in a large bowl with all the other ingredients. Stir well and leave to stand overnight in a cool place. In the morning put the mixture into a preserving pan and bring it gently to boiling point. Boil steadily for three quarters of an hour, remove the ginger and bottle up.

Bilberry Jam

The berries can be used to make a delicious jam, using a pound of preserving sugar to each pound of fruit. It is better to mix bilberries with other tart fruits (apples, redcurrants, rhubarb) to improve the setting qualities of the jam. Boil the fruit with the sugar and just enough water to cover for about twenty minutes, or until the jam sets when tested on a cold saucer. Put into clean pots and seal down.

Quick Raspberry Jam

1lb raspberries   1¼lb lump sugar

Put the raspberries in a well-buttered preserving pan. Bruise them, add the sugar and bruise again. Bring them to the boil and boil for five minutes only, then cool, pot and seal in the usual way.

Raspberry Cheese

3lb raspberries   8oz butter
4 eggs   2lb sugar

Simmer the raspberries in a very little water until soft, then rub through a sieve. Put the puree in a bowl over simmering water and add the butter and the sugar. Stir until melted, then add the beaten eggs. Stir constantly over a gentle heat until thick. A little orange juice added with the eggs will improve the flavour.

Raspberry Jam

Pick over and weigh the raspberries, and have ready the same weight in sugar. Put the fruit into a preserving pan with a quarter of the sugar and bring gently to the boil, stirring all the time with a wooden spoon. Add the remainder of the sugar and boil fast for ten minutes. This jam sets well and keeps a fine colour.

Pickles

Pickled Plums

4lb plums	6 cloves
4lb loaf sugar	¾ pint vinegar
3 sticks cinnamon	

Choose firm, ripe plums; wipe them well and prick them all over with a fork. Put all the ingredients except the plums in a large pan and bring slowly to the boil, stirring until all the sugar is dissolved to a syrup. Add the prepared plums, and stand over a low heat for ten minutes. Allow the plums to cool completely in the pan, then bottle and cover closely.

Pickled Walnuts

Prepare the walnuts by piercing them through with a darning needle. Throw away any which are too hard to be punctured. Cover the walnuts with a brine solution made by dissolving six ounces of salt in a quart of boiling water, and let them soak for six days, stirring often. Repeat the process with fresh brine for a further six days. Then drain the walnuts and spread them out on a large dish in the sun. After a few hours they will have all turned quite black, and are ready for pickling. Pack them into jars and cover with spiced vinegar. Keep for three months before using.

Sweet Pickle

2lb apples	1 teaspoon ground ginger
2lb onions	1 pint vinegar
½lb stoned raisins	½ teaspoon each salt and
½lb brown sugar	pepper

Peel and slice the apples, and chop the onions and the raisins. Put all the ingredients into a large pan and bring them gently to the boil, stirring often. Simmer for one hour, then cool and bottle.

Spiced Vinegar

1 quart malt vinegar	¼ oz peppercorns
1 oz bruised ginger	¼ oz mace
8 cloves	2 inches stick cinnamon
¼ oz whole allspice	

Tie all the spices loosely in a muslin bag, and immerse them in the vinegar. Bring to the boil slowly and gently, keeping the pan covered. Simmer for ten minutes, then allow to cool, but do not remove the spices until the vinegar is quite cold.

Pickled Onions

2 quarts small onions or shallots	½ cupful of salt
½ oz mixed allspice, cloves and peppercorns	½ cupful of sugar
	¼ pure malt vinegar

Peel the onions, put them in a basin, sprinkle over the salt, and leave to stand overnight. The following day, rinse them in plenty of water and dry as well as possible. Put the sugar, vinegar, salt and spices into a large pan, bring to the boil and simmer for five minutes. Add the onions for a further minute. Pack the onions tightly into jars and fill up to the top with the vinegar. Cover when cold. Ready to eat in two weeks.

To Pickle a Tongue

Put half a pound of salt, two ounces of sugar, and half an ounce of saltpetre in a jug. Pour over them two gills of boiling water and allow to cool. When completely cold, immerse the tongue in the liquid and let it remain there for fourteen days, turning every day.

Green Gooseberry Chutney

2lbs green gooseberries	1 pint vinegar
1lb onions	1 teaspoon salt
1lb raisins	1 teaspoon ground ginger
6oz sugar	½ teaspoon cayenne pepper

Top and tail the gooseberries, chop the onions and the raisins. Combine all the ingredients and boil very gently for at least one hour. This chutney keeps well and is delicious with cold meats.

Yorkshire Relish

2 pints malt vinegar	pinch of cayenne pepper
8oz brown sugar	1 teaspoon pickling spice
1½oz pearl barley	1 teaspoon spanish juice
pinch of salt	

Put all the ingredients in a pan, bring slowly to the boil, stirring until the sugar is dissolved. Simmer gently for three-quarters of an hour, then cool and bottle.

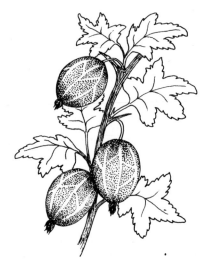

Drinks

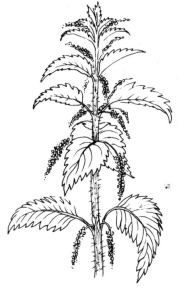

Nettle Beer

Gather enough tender young nettle tops to fill a large basket, taking care to wear good thick gloves. Put them in a large pan with enough water to cover, taken from four quarts, and boil until soft and tender. Strain off the liquid into a large bowl, add the rest of the water together with half a pound of sugar and two lemons cut into slices. When the liquid has cooled to blood heat, add one ounce of yeast and leave overnight. The following morning the beer is ready to be strained and bottled. The addition of the following mixture will improve the drink, but it is not essential:

Half a teaspoon of bicarbonate of soda

Half a teaspoon of tartaric acid

Beat these together with a little white of **egg**, and stir into the beer before bottling.

Elderberry Wine

1 quart elderberries	1 piece root ginger
1lb Valencia raisins	½oz yeast
1lb sugar	3 pints water

Chop the raisins and put these in a large pan with the elderberries and the ginger root. Pour over three pints of water and bring to the boil. Simmer for half an hour, then add the sugar, stir well and allow to cool. When the mixture is just lukewarm, stir in the yeast. Leave to stand overnight, then strain and bottle. Ready in three months.

Cleat Wine

'Cleat' is the local name for the Coltsfoot, a small yellow flower often found growing on waste land. It blooms early in the spring, usually in March.

Take one pint of Cleat heads pressed down, and pour a gallon of boiling water over them. When it has cooled, strain off the liquid and boil for twenty minutes with three pounds of brown sugar. Have a large bowl ready, and into it put two unpeeled oranges, cut into quarters; the rind of two lemons, and a pound of large stoneless raisins, chopped finely. Pour the boiling liquid over these and when it has cooled, add the juice of two lemons. Finally, spread two ounces of yeast on a piece of toast, and add this also. Allow it to work for three days, then strain and put into bottles. Do not screw the tops down too tightly at first.

Dandelion Wine

Best in early summer when the gleaming gold flowers are at their most profuse. Gather the flower heads only without any stalk, although a few scrubbed roots may be added to strengthen the flavour of the wine.

To every quart of flowers add three quarts of boiling water. Let them stand for one week, and give them a good stir every day. Then add an orange and two lemons cut into thin slices, and leave to stand for another week. The liquid is then ready to be strained off and measured; add a pound of demerara sugar to every quart. Leave for another twenty-four hours, stirring frequently. The wine is then ready to be bottled, and should be left in a cool dark place for a few months before drinking.

Ginger Beer

Take three tablespoons sugar, half a large teaspoon of tartaric acid powder, and one teaspoon of liquid Jamaica Ginger. Let the ginger be good and strong. Dissolve the ingredients in three pints of boiling water, then allow to stand for a day in a cool place. This enjoyable summer drink does not effervesce and needs no bottling.

Lemon Syrup

Take the juice and outer rind of three lemons, together with two pounds of sugar, and pour over them one and half pints of boiling water. Leave until cold and then stir in one ounce of citric acid, dissolved in a cup of cold water. Mix well, strain and bottle. Dilute with cool water for a refreshing drink.

Elderflower Drink

Put six large elderflower sprigs in a large jug, together with one tablespoon of white wine vinegar, three-quarters of a pound of sugar, and the juice and rind of two lemons. Pour two quarts of water over all and allow to stand for at least thirty-six hours. Strain and bottle the drink and then let it stand for a week or two.

Elderberry Syrup

Pick as many ripe clusters of elderberries as will fill a large pan. Add just enough water to cover them and bring slowly to the boil, then simmer until the berries are soft and pulpy. Strain through a sieve to remove all the stalks, and then measure the strained syrup. Return it to the pan with half a pound of sugar to every pint of liquid, adding half an ounce of cloves and a bruised ginger root. Simmer for half an hour, and then allow to cool before bottling. Generally used for coughs and colds; take two tablespoonsful in a large cup of hot water.

Gruel

This used to be considered very valuable for a nursing mother.

4 tablespoons oatmeal	1 tablespoon salt
2 tablespoons sugar	½ teaspoon ginger

Pour a quart of boiling water over the ingredients, stir and leave to stand for an hour in a cool place. Then strain into a pan, bring to the boil and cook gently for a few minutes. Serve with a little milk added.

Raspberry Vinegar

Take two or three quarts of fresh raspberries, put them in a stoneware crock or glass bowl and cover with best white malt vinegar. Leave them for a week, stirring gently from time to time. Then strain them through a jelly bag, without squeezing, until all the juice is extracted. Measure a pound of sugar to each pint of juice, and heat gently in a preserving pan until the sugar has dissolved. Boil briskly for ten minutes, then allow to cool before bottling. Use diluted with hot water as a soothing drink for sore throats in winter. It may also be sprinkled on Yorkshire pudding immediately before serving.

Blackberry Vinegar

Make this in exactly the same way as the Raspberry Vinegar above, using the sweet early-ripened berries. (October blackberries are more bitter). A tablespoonful in hot water makes a particularly comforting drink to relieve a cold in the head.

Pobs

Sometimes called 'Possets', this was a simple dish for invalids or for children at supper time.

three or four slices of old bread   ½ pint milk
one tablespoon treacle

Trim the crusts from the bread and cut it into cubes. Warm the milk and treacle, and pour it over the bread, so that it is well soaked. Serve while it is hot.

Aunt Martha Ann's Cure for a Cough

Put two clean eggs into a basin with the shells on, just as they are. Squeeze three lemons over them and let them stand for three days and nights with a plate on top, then strain through muslin. Add one pennyworth of sugar candy broken in bits and add a gill of best Jamaica rum. Stir well together and pour into bottles.

Metric Equivalents

¼oz	7g	1lb	454g
½oz	14g	2lb	907g
¾oz	21g	3lb	1.36kg
1oz	28g		
4oz (¼lb)	113g	¼ pint (1 gill)	142ml
8oz (½lb)	227g	½ pint	283ml
12oz (¾lb)	340g	1 pint	576ml

Index

64